Francis Frith's
AROUND BLACKPOOL

PHOTOGRAPHIC MEMORIES

Francis Frith's
AROUND BLACKPOOL

◆

Clive Hardy

First published in the United Kingdom in 1999 by
Frith Book Company Ltd

Hardback Edition
ISBN 1-85937-049-7

Paperback Edition 2001
ISBN 1-85937-382-8

British Library Cataloguing in Publication Data

Francis Frith's Around Blackpool
Clive Hardy

Frith Book Company Ltd
Frith's Barn, Teffont,
Salisbury, Wiltshire SP3 5QP
Tel: +44 (0) 1722 716 376
Email: info@francisfrith.co.uk
www.francisfrith.co.uk

Printed and bound in Great Britain

AS WITH ANY HISTORICAL DATABASE THE FRITH ARCHIVE IS CONSTANTLY BEING CORRECTED AND IMPROVED
AND THE PUBLISHERS WOULD WELCOME INFORMATION ON OMISSIONS OR INACCURACIES

Contents

FRANCIS FRITH: *Victorian Pioneer*

FRANCIS FRITH, Victorian founder of the world-famous photographic archive, was a complex and multitudinous man. A devout Quaker and a highly successful Victorian businessman, he was both philosophic by nature and pioneering in outlook.

By 1855 Francis Frith had already established a wholesale grocery business in Liverpool, and sold it for the astonishing sum of £200,000, which is the equivalent today of over £15,000,000. Now a multi-millionaire, he was able to indulge his passion for travel. As a child he had pored over travel books written by early explorers, and his fancy and imagination had been stirred by family holidays to the sublime mountain regions of Wales and Scotland. 'What a land of spirit-stirring and enriching scenes and places!' he had written. He was to return to these scenes of grandeur in later years to 'recapture the thousands of vivid and tender memories', but with a different purpose. Now in his thirties, and captivated by the new science of photography, Frith set out on a series of pioneering journeys to the Nile regions that occupied him from 1856 until 1860.

INTRIGUE AND ADVENTURE

He took with him on his travels a specially-designed wicker carriage that acted as both dark-room and sleeping chamber. These far-flung journeys were packed with intrigue and adventure. In his life story, written when he was sixty-three, Frith tells of being held captive by bandits, and of fighting 'an awful midnight battle to the very point of surrender with a deadly pack of hungry, wild dogs'. Sporting flowing Arab costume, Frith arrived at Akaba by camel seventy years before Lawrence, where he encountered 'desert princes and rival sheikhs, blazing with jewel-hilted swords'.

During these extraordinary adventures he was assiduously exploring the desert regions bordering the Nile and patiently recording the antiquities and peoples with his camera. He was the first photographer to venture beyond the sixth cataract. Africa was still the mysterious 'Dark Continent', and Stanley and Livingstone's historic meeting was a decade into the future. The conditions for picture taking confound belief. He laboured for hours in his wicker dark-room in the sweltering heat of the desert, while the volatile chemicals fizzed dangerously in their trays. Often he was forced to work in remote tombs and caves

where conditions were cooler. Back in London he exhibited his photographs and was 'rapturously cheered' by members of the Royal Society. His reputation as a photographer was made overnight. An eminent modern historian has likened their impact on the population of the time to that on our own generation of the first photographs taken on the surface of the moon.

VENTURE OF A LIFE-TIME

Characteristically, Frith quickly spotted the opportunity to create a new business as a specialist publisher of photographs. He lived in an era of immense and sometimes violent change. For the poor in the early part of Victoria's reign work was a drudge and the hours long, and people had precious little free time to enjoy themselves.

Most had no transport other than a cart or gig at their disposal, and had not travelled far beyond the boundaries of their own town or village. However, by the 1870s, the railways had threaded their way across the country, and Bank Holidays and half-day Saturdays had been made obligatory by Act of Parliament. All of a sudden the ordinary working man and his family were able to enjoy days out and see a little more of the world.

With characteristic business acumen, Francis Frith foresaw that these new tourists would enjoy having souvenirs to commemorate their days out. In 1860 he married Mary Ann Rosling and set out with the intention of photographing every city, town and village in Britain. For the next thirty years he travelled the country by train and by pony and trap, producing fine photographs of seaside resorts and beauty spots that were keenly bought by millions of Victorians. These prints were painstakingly pasted into family albums and pored over during the dark nights of winter, rekindling precious memories of summer excursions.

THE RISE OF FRITH & CO

Frith's studio was soon supplying retail shops all over the country. To meet the demand he gathered about him a small team of photographers, and published the work of independent artist-photographers of the calibre of Roger Fenton and Francis Bedford. In order to gain some understanding of the scale of Frith's business one only has to look at the catalogue issued by Frith & Co in 1886: it runs to some 670

pages, listing not only many thousands of views of the British Isles but also many photographs of most European countries, and China, Japan, the USA and Canada – note the sample page shown above from the hand-written *Frith & Co* ledgers detailing pictures taken. By 1890 Frith had created the greatest specialist photographic publishing company in the world, with over 2,000 outlets – more than the combined number that Boots and WH Smith have today! The picture on the right shows the *Frith & Co* display board at Ingleton in the Yorkshire Dales. Beautifully constructed with mahogany frame and gilt inserts, it could display up to a dozen local scenes.

POSTCARD BONANZA

The ever-popular holiday postcard we know today took many years to develop. In 1870 the Post Office issued the first plain cards, with a pre-printed stamp on one face. In 1894 they allowed other publishers' cards to be sent through the mail with an attached adhesive halfpenny stamp. Demand grew rapidly, and in 1895 a new size of postcard was permitted called the

court card, but there was little room for illustration. In 1899, a year after Frith's death, a new card measuring 5.5 x 3.5 inches became the standard format, but it was not until 1902 that the divided back came into being, with address and message on one face and a full-size illustration on the other. *Frith & Co* were in the vanguard of postcard development, and Frith's sons Eustace and Cyril continued their father's monumental task, expanding the number of views offered to the public and recording more and more places in Britain, as the coasts and countryside were opened up to mass travel.

Francis Frith died in 1898 at his villa in Cannes, his great project still growing. The archive he created continued in business for another seventy years. By 1970 it contained over a third of a million pictures of 7,000 cities, towns and villages. The massive photographic record Frith has left to us stands as a living monument to a special and very remarkable man.

Frith's Archive: *A Unique Legacy*

FRANCIS FRITH'S legacy to us today is of immense significance and value, for the magnificent archive of evocative photographs he created provides a unique record of change in 7,000 cities, towns and villages throughout Britain over a century and more. Frith and his fellow studio photographers revisited locations many times down the years to update their views, compiling for us an enthralling and colourful pageant of British life and character.

We tend to think of Frith's sepia views of Britain as nostalgic, for most of us use them to conjure up memories of places in our own lives with which we have family associations. It often makes us forget that to Francis Frith they were records of daily life as it was actually being lived in the cities, towns and villages of his day. The Victorian age was one of great and often bewildering change for ordinary people, and though the pictures evoke an impression of slower times, life was as busy and hectic as it is today.

We are fortunate that Frith was a photographer of the people, dedicated to recording the minutiae of everyday life. For it is this sheer wealth of visual data, the painstaking chronicle of changes in dress, transport, street layouts, buildings, housing, engineering and landscape that captivates us so much today. His remarkable images offer us a powerful link with the past and with the lives of our ancestors.

TODAY'S TECHNOLOGY

Computers have now made it possible for Frith's many thousands of images to be accessed almost instantly. In the Frith archive today, each photograph is carefully 'digitised' then stored on a CD Rom. Frith archivists can locate a single photograph amongst thousands within seconds. Views can be catalogued and sorted under a variety of categories of place and content to the immediate benefit of researchers. Inexpensive reference prints can be created for them at the touch of a mouse button, and a wide range of books and other printed materials assembled and published for a wider, more general readership - in the next twelve months over a hundred Frith local history titles will be published! The

THE FRANCIS FRITH COLLECTION
Photographic publishers since 1860

HOME | PHOTO SEARCH | BOOKS | PORTFOLIO | GALLERY | MY CART
Products | History | Other Collections | Contact us | Help?

your town,
your village

365,000
photographs of 7,000 towns and villages, taken between 1860 & 1970.

The Frith Archive
The Frith Archive is the remarkable legacy of its energetic and visionary founder. Today, the Frith archive is the only nationally important archive of its kind still in private ownership.

The Collection is world-renowned for the extraordinary quality of its images.

The Gallery
This month The Frith Gallery features images from "Frith's Egypt".

*the*FRITHgallery

News...

Image update complete.
An additional 5,000 images have been added and the quality of all images has now been improved.

Sample Chapters avaliable.
The first selection of sample chapters from the Frith Book Co.'s extensive range is now available. All are offered in Pdf format for easy downloading and viewing.

explore
FRITH
Search thousands of photographs from one of the worlds' great archives.

Town search

GO

County search
Select a county

GO

See Frith at www. francisfrith.co.uk

day-to-day workings of the archive are very different from how they were in Francis Frith's time: imagine the herculean task of sorting through eleven tons of glass negatives as Frith had to do to locate a particular sequence of pictures! Yet the archive still prides itself on maintaining the same high standards of excellence laid down by Francis Frith, including the painstaking cataloguing and indexing of every view.

It is curious to reflect on how the internet now allows researchers in America and elsewhere greater instant access to the archive than Frith himself ever enjoyed. Many thousands of individual views can be called up on screen within seconds on one of the Frith internet sites, enabling people living continents away to revisit the streets of their ancestral home town, or view places in Britain where they have enjoyed holidays. Many overseas researchers welcome the chance to view special theme selections, such as transport, sports, costume and ancient monuments.

We are certain that Francis Frith would have heartily approved of these modern developments, for he himself was always working at the very limits of Victorian photographic technology.

THE VALUE OF THE ARCHIVE TODAY

Because of the benefits brought by the computer, Frith's images are increasingly studied by social historians, by researchers into genealogy and ancestory, by architects, town planners, and by teachers and schoolchildren involved in local history projects. In addition, the archive offers every one of us a unique opportunity to examine the places where we and our families have lived and worked down the years. Immensely successful in Frith's own era, the archive is now, a century and more on, entering a new phase of popularity.

THE PAST IN TUNE WITH THE FUTURE

Historians consider the Francis Frith Collection to be of prime national importance. It is the only archive of its kind remaining in private ownership and has been valued at a million pounds. However, this figure is now rapidly increasing as digital technology enables more and more people around the world to enjoy its benefits.

Francis Frith's archive is now housed in an historic timber barn in the beautiful village of Teffont in Wiltshire. Its founder would not recognize the archive office as it is today. In place of the many thousands of dusty boxes containing glass plate negatives and an all-pervading odour of photographic chemicals, there are now ranks of computer screens. He would be amazed to watch his images travelling round the world at unimaginable speeds through network and internet lines.

The archive's future is both bright and exciting. Francis Frith, with his unshakeable belief in making photographs available to the greatest number of people, would undoubtedly approve of what is being done today with his lifetime's work. His photographs, depicting our shared past, are now bringing pleasure and enlightenment to millions around the world a century and more after his death.

BLACKPOOL – *An Introduction*

THE EARLY YEARS

The first reference to Blackpool that we have with any certainty appears in the Bispham Church register for 1602, recording the christening of 'Ellen Cowban, daughter of Thomas Cowban of blackpoole'. And that is precisely what the place was; a black pool, near the mouth of the Spen, its waters coloured by the peaty moss through which it flowed. The area was remote, marshy and windswept, and was a part of Lancashire known as Agmunderness, whose main townships included Poulton, Rossall, Bispham, Lytham, Thornton and Inskip. When Ellen was alive, most people along this part of the coast lived in single-storied cottages built with arched timbers (crooks), wattle and clay walls, and thatch made from rushes.

One of the first houses of any substance to be built near the black pool was Fox Hall. It is said that around the year 1655 Edward Tyldesley, a member of a Catholic pro-Royalist family, whose seat was at Myerscough Hall, near Garstang, built Fox Hall as a summer residence. An alternative theory is that given the Hall's remote location, it was, in fact, used as

a base for pro-Royalist activities, and that Charles II may well have been a regular visitor in the years before the Restoration. The Hall was close enough to the sea to allow the King a chance of escape should the need arise. Fox Hall was eventually abandoned by the Tyldesleys and, after being used as a farm, was converted into an inn; alas, nothing remains of the original building.

In 1751, Blackpool as a town in its own right appears on a map, thanks to the cartographer Emmanuel Bowen who recorded the place as Black Pool Town. There wasn't much to see, perhaps twenty or thirty cottages, but it was a start, and the craze for sea-bathing was gaining momentum. By the end of the 1750s Black Pool Town consisted of cottages, the Gynn Inn, two hotels and Fox Hall. It was in the 1780s that the area became a fashionable haunt for the sea-bathing set. In 1784 a summer season coach service operated from the Lower Swan Inn, Manchester, every Monday, Wednesday and Friday. The journey took about twelve hours; the inside fare was 14s, and a meal stop was made at the Black Bull Inn, Preston. Most of the inhabitants, however, continued to earn their living either labouring on the land, or fishing, or both.

One story about the village goes back to the year 1799 when the Lancashire potato crop failed, and the corn harvest was so poor that prices rocketed. On top of this, a freak storm broke along the coast, wrecking fishing boats, flooding inland and destroying or damaging many of the cottages. The people of Blackpool were now facing winter with little or no food reserves, and were unable to meet the prices being demanded inland. But salvation comes in many forms. As the storm destroyed their homes and livelihoods, it also carried with it a merchantship, sails torn away and rudder smashed. Despite their own suffering, men made their way down to the beach to try and help the crew of the stricken ship, which by now was aground and in danger of breaking up. Then from nowhere a giant wave lifted the vessel bodily and brought it further up the beach, enabling the crew to be rescued before she broke up. Amid the debris were barrels, sacks and packages. It turned out that her cargo was mainly provisions, the bulk of it peas. The people of Blackpool survived the winter of 1799-1800

on a diet of peas, fish and cockles.

By the time the railway arrived in Blackpool in 1846, the town was already a resort attracting several thousand visitors a year. Baileys Hotel, later the Metropole, had opened in 1776. The first bathing-machines had been imported by an enterprising inn keeper as early as 1730, though whether or not they were available for hire on Sundays, as the two machines at Lytham were, so that the frail could be trundled to and from church, is unknown. One of the earliest attractions was Uncle Tom's Cabin, which started out as little more than a wooden hut from which Thomas Parkinson sold sweetmeats and ginger beer during the summer season. Parkinson appears to have gone under the name of 'Uncle Tom', hence the name of Uncle Tom's Cabin.

Eventually Parkinson sold out to a man named Taylor. He went into partnership with another man in order to develop the business, but they did turn down the chance to buy the field the cabin stood in, and the one next to it, for just £15. Fate now plays its hand. Some time after Taylor had taken over, a wooden bust of a negro, thought to be a ship's figurehead, was washed ashore. By coincidence, one of the best-selling books of the time was 'Uncle Tom's Cabin', so Taylor simply stuck the figurehead on the roof, and added those of Eva and Topsy, implying that the cabin was in fact named after the hero of the book.

During the 1830s Blackpool was still developing along genteel lines, though it must be said that for several decades the tradition of the Lancashire working people and their families visiting the town had already begun, albeit on a small scale. Many would make the journey by cart; some would even walk, just to spend a few hours away from the dust, grit, grime and monotony of mill and factory life. Some resorts simply didn't want the lower social orders at play; the Yorkshire spa Scarborough even issued a broadsheet stating that 'the watering place has no wish for a greater influx of vagrants and those who have no money to spend'. The Scarborough broadsheet was also an attack on the railways, the very mode of transport that would bring both it, and the likes of Blackpool and Southport, much of their wealth.

VICTORIAN DEVELOPMENT

By the 1870s many Lancashire cotton workers were enjoying the luxury of three unpaid days' holiday a year, which when tacked onto a weekend gave a handy five-day break. Another important development for Blackpool's holiday industry was the passing of the Bank Holidays Act in 1871. With specific days allocated for holidays, the railway companies could schedule special excursion trains knowing that they would be filled. With the railway, investment in Blackpool's infrastructure and attractions gathered momentum. The North Pier opened in 1863 and was followed by a second, the South Jetty, in 1868. In 1879 electric lighting was introduced along the promenade and the first illuminated tramcars ran as early as 1897, inspired, it is said, by the Kaiser's birthday celebrations in Berlin.

While Scarborough, Southport and Morecambe continued to provide for the genteel classes, Blackpool was developing along more gregarious lines. When they were opened in 1878, the Winter Gardens were probably the town's last throw at catering for a sophisticated audience. They housed a library, reading room, art gallery and concert hall. But the writing was on the wall as early as Whit weekend 1879, when the Garden's principal attraction was a young lady being fired from a cannon. As the popularity of the Gardens grew, so Uncle Tom's Cabin declined, despite the fact that it too had its own dance orchestra. For Uncle Tom's the end would come in 1906; not the victim of financial circumstances, but of nature itself, when cliff erosion caused a part of the buildings to collapse.

In September 1885, Blackpool opened the first fare-paying street-tramway in the country to be equipped with electric cars. Initially the tramway was confined to the promenade, where it ran over a two-mile single line, with passing loops every three hundred yards. The trams were powered by what was known as the conduit system, a positive current being carried by copper conductors in a central channel between the tracks. The cars were fitted with a shoe, which fitted into the conduit and made contact with the conductors, thereby picking up the current. The cars were capable of speeds in excess of 15mph, but were, in fact, restricted by an interfering Board of Trade to 8mph. Though successful, the system had its drawbacks in that the conduit was prone to loss of current due to its filling with sea water or drifting sand. The Corporation took over the line in 1892 and converted it to overhead wire in 1898-99.

In 1894 Blackpool pulled off the seaside coup of the century with the opening of the Tower. Blackpool has never been shy of borrowing good ideas from elsewhere. At 518ft high, the Tower was based on that in Paris. As the crowds flocked in to see this engineering masterpiece, other resorts announced their intentions to build their own towers; but only Morecambe and New Brighton ever got anywhere. The Tower was followed in 1899 with the opening of the Tower Ballroom, modelled on the Paris Opera House, and famed for its mighty Wurlitzer organ which would feature in countless BBC broadcasts and make organist Reginald Dixon a household name.

By the beginning of the 20th century Blackpool was the preferred holiday destination for the majority of Lancashire cotton workers, but it was also drawing in holiday-makers from as far afield as Scotland, the Midlands and the North East. During Wakes Week, 1919, no less than 10,000 people from Nelson stayed in Blackpool, while just 1,000 headed off to Southport and around 500 went to the Isle of Man, via Fleetwood. The town became adept at handling large influxes of people. On Bank Holiday Monday in August 1937, no less than 425 special trains ran to Blackpool and, over the bank holiday period, the town is said to have had five million visitors. True or not, we do know that on one day in July 1945 over 100,000 people came to the town by train.

The 1920 Dunlop Guide describes Blackpool as 'the most popular seaside resort in England: scene of the holiday revels of Manchester, Liverpool, and the industrial centres of Lancashire generally. Blackpool has gone into the 'business' of catering for the millions exactly as into a business, and it was the pioneer in the advertising of local attractions, having secured a local Act of Parliament authorising expenditure out of the rates for that purpose. It is a frankly democratic and by no means exclusive place, but the entertainments, of which there is an almost endless variety, are the very best of their kind. The theatres, concert halls, zoological gardens, dancing saloons or ballrooms, gardens, Eiffel Tower, and other ingenious attractions are maintained with the most lavish expenditure of money. The site of Blackpool, a little over a century ago, was a sandy waste, and the town is scarce half-a-century old'.

While Blackpool followed the pack-them-in-and-give-them-what-they-want road, Lytham St Annes and Southport became popular residential areas for Lancashire businessmen. It allowed them to appear prosperous, as indeed many of them were, without overdoing it. In B Bowker's book 'Lancashire under the Hammer', he relates the story of a weaver who married his boss's daughter in 1908 and went to work at the Manchester Exchange, where he sold yarn on a fixed commission rate of half a per cent. Within four years the ex-weaver had made enough money to buy a house in Southport. By 1920 he had made over £150,000 and had moved into a large house at St Annes. Lytham's development was due to the influence of the Clifton family, who owned more than 15,000 acres in southwest Lancashire; most of it was acquired at the time of the Dissolution. St Annes was to be the last of the Fylde resorts to be developed, and would eventually be joined to Lytham.

THE GOLDEN MILE

Eager for new attractions guaranteed to pull in the crowds, the Corporation organized an Aviation Week in October 1909. What we have to remember in 1999 is that ninety years ago, flying was an 'in' thing. In 1909 Louis Bleriot caused a sensation when he successfully flew across the English Channel, and the aviators of his day were idolized, much the same as rock and film stars are today. Thousands came to Blackpool to watch pilots and aircraft compete in races for prize money ranging from £50 to £2,000. The event was repeated in 1910. When Graham White landed his plane on the beach near the Victoria Pier, hundreds of spectators scrambled for a chance to touch the machine. Thousands watched from the beach and the Golden Mile as a French aviator flew around and over the Tower, and another pilot broke the world height record by flying at more than one mile high.

In 1910 the Corporation evicted a gipsy camp on the South Shore, as the site was being redeveloped as the Pleasure Beach. As early as 1907 Blackpool had opened a scenic railway, the first of its type in the UK, though already popular in amusement parks in the United States. The Casino opened in 1913 and included a restaurant, cinema and billiard hall, and when the Big Dipper was built in 1923 at a cost of £25,000 it set in motion the trend by which the Pleasure Beach Company continues to invest in new and exciting rides.

As early as 1919, the Golden Mile was awash with sideshows and paper hats bearing that well-known legend 'Kiss Me Quick'. It was all a part of the atmosphere, bordering on the naughty, but not quite getting there. In the late 1930s Blackpool's reputation as an 'anything goes' place was the subject of a Mass Observation survey after seventy-six babies were born in the town out of wedlock in 1936. But of the 400 or so couples caught in the middle of the night on the beach, or under the piers, only four couples were engaged in anything other than holding hands or kissing. Of the four couples, one included a member of the Mass Observation, who was obviously doing his bit to bump up the statistics!

Blackpool's reputation was due mainly to the likes of showmen like Luke Gannon, who would try almost anything once. In the 1930s Luke Gannon offered the Reverend Harold Davidson, the defrocked Rector of Stiffkey, £100 a week to live in a barrel on the Golden Mile. The Rector had been thrown out of the Church for ministering unto young ladies in ways other than spiritual. His defence was made all the harder when the prosecution got its hands on several pictures of Davidson cavorting naked with the ladies in question. Sandwiched between a fasting girl and a flea circus, Davidson sat in his barrel expounding on the injustice of his situation. In August 1938, Davidson's final demonstration of his innocence was to appear at Skegness among the lions of a travelling menagerie. He was a sort of latter-day Daniel in the lions' den - but a lion ate him. Hundreds attended his funeral and fought one another for handfuls of earth from his grave.

During the summer of 1938, Gannon had the punters paying 2d a time to see the newly wedded Colonel and Mrs Barker lying in separate beds, their marriage as yet unconsummated. The Colonel was supposed to have been born a woman, and had undergone the world's first sex change operation to become a fully functioning male. The reason the two were lying there was said to be for a bet; the Colonel stood to win £250 if he could keep his new-found manhood to himself for twenty-one weeks. It was all a con. At night, when our love-sick couple were supposedly being monitored by Gannon's ever vigilant staff, the

Colonel, who was a man, was at home with his mistress, while his 'wife' went off to her digs. Blackpool continues to attract large numbers of visitors, despite the competition from package holidays and last-minute deals by travel agents. The Pleasure Gardens prides itself on its spectacular rides, and seems to be locked in some kind of duel with Alton Towers to come up with the most hair-raising. The trams continue to run, and the Tower is still standing; other places would have almost certainly got rid of both of them in the so-called name of progress. If you have never been to Blackpool, don't knock it until you have tried it.

FLEETWOOD

Fleetwood was founded in 1836 by Sir Peter Hesketh-Fleetwood, and was laid out to the designs of Decimus Burton, who designed the North Euston Hotel, Queen's Terrace and both lighthouses.

They planned that the town would be a little way inland and separate from the dock area. For a short time Fleetwood was, in effect, the northern terminus of the London & North Western Railway line from Euston, and the connecting stop for steamer services to and from Belfast, Ardrossan and various west coast ports. The railway reached Fleetwood in July 1840, six years before it reached Blackpool.

The line was a single track and ran from Preston via Kirkham, Poulton and Thornton. Fleetwood lacked the infrastructure to compete with Liverpool as a major port for passenger and cargo traffic, but it did become England's principal fishing port on the west coast, with a fleet to rival those of Hull and Grimsby. The advantage that Fleetwood had

as a port was that its entrance channel was free of hazards to navigation such as sandbars and moving banks. Even at low tide, vessels drawing less than sixteen feet of water could manoeuvre within the harbour basin, and boats drawing less than five feet could still use the channel.

A 1906 tour guide describes Fleetwood as,'a flourishing watering-place on the Irish Channel. Mail steamers ply hence daily to Belfast, and there is a summer-service to the Isle of Man. About 3m to the S.W. is Rossall School, a large public school (400 boys)'. Rossall Hall had been the home of Sir Hesketh-Fleetwood, and became a school in 1844.

LYTHAM & ST ANNE'S

Lytham was to develop on somewhat more genteel lines than Blackpool, owing to the influence of the Clifton family who owned over 15,000 acres in southwest Lancashire. Their land in Lytham had been acquired at the time of the Dissolution when they purchased the estates of the former Benedictine priory.

There were two bathing machines at Lytham by the mid-1730s. The added bonus was that they were available for hire on Sundays, so that those of a more frail disposition might be trundled to church and back. St Anne's was the last of the Fylde resorts to be developed, and though it would eventually join with Lytham to form the Borough of Lytham St Anne's, it was originally a separate Urban District. The town was laid out in the garden city fashion and, as in Lytham and Southport, merchants, mill owners and manufacturers soon took up residence.

UNCLE TOM'S CABIN 1906 53875

In its heyday, Uncle Tom's Cabin offered dancing to its own orchestra, refreshments, and American Portraits 'taken and finished while you wait'. On the roof are three wooden figures representing Uncle Tom, Eva and Topsy. Shortly after this picture was taken in 1906, cliff erosion caused a part of the building to collapse; the remainder was demolished in 1907.

NORTH PROMENADE 1906 53874

A Dreadnought tramcar approaches the terminus at Queen's Gate. At this time the Blackpool and Fleetwood tramway systems were separate concerns, and even lacked a connecting line. Those wishing to continue north had to walk a few yards to the Fleetwood terminus and join a tram there.

NORTH SHORE C1955 B116014
The cliff walk along the North Shore. The walk features heavily in the annual illuminations; many of the set pieces
are erected along it.

CLIFF WALK, NORTH SHORE C1955 B116022
The cliff walk and the Gynn tram stop. The Gynn was a busy junction in the heyday of the tramway system. There
was a line from here to the North Station, and it was also here that the trams belonging to Lytham St Anne's
Corporation terminated.

NORTH SHORE
1890 22886
Bathing machines await customers. A typical machine had
a door and a pair of shafts at either end. The lady would
enter from the landward side, whilst the horse was
attached to the seaward end. Once in the water, the lady,
suitably attired to protect her modesty, would leave the
machine and bathe.

THE IMPERIAL HYDROPATHIC ESTABLISHMENT 1890 22890

The hydropathic craze swept Britain from the 1840s onwards, when a German practitioner named Vincenz Priessnitz developed a series of treatments using ordinary cold water, thus saving the need to visit a spa town. There were dozens of treatments, some including the use of electricity.

CLAREMONT PARK TERRACE 1890 22889

This view also shows the Imperial Hydropathic Hotel. Hydros were for the more affluent visitor, charging anything between 8s 6d and 10s 6d per day, with treatments extra. Among the facilities at places like the Norbeck Hall Hydro were tennis courts and an indoor swimming pool.

NORTH PROMENADE 1906

The North Promenade offered walkways on different levels. Here residents from the hydropathic establishments could avail themselves of a pre-dinner constitutional and take in the bracing sea air. The hydropathic regime consisted of exercise, water treatments and regulated diets; hydros weren't too keen on alcohol either.

◆

THE TERRACE 1890

Is this family smiling for the camera, or have they noticed that little Johnny, head down and pedalling like mad, is on a collision course with our man from Frith? Apart from that, notice the old cottage between the two terraces.

NORTH PROMENADE 1906 53873

THE TERRACE 1890 22887

LOWER PROMENADE, NORTH SHORE C1955 B116019
Though most of the people appear to be well wrapped-up against the onshore breeze, there are plenty of takers for a paddle or a swim.

TALBOT SQUARE 1890 22893
On the left is the ornate drinking fountain, while over on the right is one of the town's earliest theatres, the Theatre Royal, which opened in 1868. Talbot Road was developed by Thomas Clifton to link his estate at Layton with the Promenade. When he died, Thomas bequeathed Talbot Square to the town.

NORTH PIER AND FOUNTAIN 1890 22879
This view is taken from Talbot Square. The oldest of the town's three piers, this one dates from 1863, and when it opened was known simply as Blackpool Pier. By that time, Blackpool's nearby rival Southport had had a pier for three years; it was 1,200 yards long and capable of handling excursion steamers.

NORTH PIER 1890 22880
The departure of an excursion steamer attracts the attention of several promenaders. At this time the longest pier in the country was at Southport, but in 1897 it was eclipsed by the pier at Southend.

FROM NORTH PIER
1906 53853
The North Pier now has its new large pavilion
straddling the entrance. We can also see something
of the new sea wall, built as Blackpool progressively
widened the Promenade from the early 1900s
onwards. Much of the work was carried out to the
plan of the then Borough Engineer, James Brodie.

THE CLIFTON HOTEL FROM THE PIER 1890 22878
A view from the North Pier towards Talbot Square. On the right is the 100-bed Clifton Hotel, an extensively rebuilt inn, originally named the Clifton Arms in honour of Thomas Clifton.

ON THE PIER 1890 22877
Out for an afternoon stroll. Notice just how immaculate the pier is: but then this was in the days before ice-cream wrappers, cola and lager cans, crisp packets, and chewing gum.

FROM NORTH PIER 1899 43330

It's 'on with the show' on the North Pier with an afternoon concert. Among the popular seaside entertainments were minstrel shows, which had originated in the USA in the early nineteenth century. The entertainers usually, but not necessarily, wore blackface makeup, sang songs and told jokes.

FROM THE PIER 1896 38839

There is a bit of a swell on, and the majority of people are wrapped up warmly. The picture gives us an indication of the size of the Gigantic Wheel at the Winter Gardens and the imposing bulk of the Tower.

FROM NORTH PIER 1906 53852
This photograph gives us a good view of the new sea wall built as part of the widening of the Promenade. In 1910, the section from North Pier round the Metropole to Cocker Street was widened; the work was completed in time for Easter 1911. The in-fill was sand, brought from the southern end of town by means of a specially laid railway line.

BAILEYS HOTEL 1895 35578

Built in 1776, the building has been enlarged and extended, and is now a part of the Metropole Hotel. It is still possible to make out a part of the building shown here by standing on the North Pier and looking at the near left-hand side and corner of the Metropole.

FROM THE SOUTH JETTY 1890 22867

Sail boats and bathing machines dominate the beach area between the North Pier and the South Jetty. In the distance we get some idea of the development of this end of the town.

THE AQUARIUM 1890 22888

A pre-Tower picture. Featured here are Dr W H Cocker's aquarium, menagerie and aviary, which occupied the site where the Tower now stands. The menagerie was retained as a Tower attraction, but it also gained fame as the setting for Stanley Holloway's monologue about young Albert Ramsbottom and the 'to do' when Albert was eaten by the menagerie lion.

FROM THE PIER 1891 29597

The sea front on a somewhat stormy day. In the centre of the picture is the Prince of Wales Theatre, one of three in the town. One of the earliest was the Borough Theatre and Concert Hall, which later became Bannisters Arcade. After a second spell as a theatre, it became the local branch of C&A.

THE SEA FRONT 1891 29594

From the same sequence as the previous storm picture, it is not too difficult to understand the operating problems the corporation experienced with its first trams, due to sea water and drifting sand getting into the conduit power supply. It was for these reasons that the system was converted to overhead power from June 1899.

THE TOWER 1896 38852A

Not much of a chance for a donkey ride on a day like this one. This photograph was taken from somewhere near the entrance to the Central Pier. The tram lines are somewhere under the water.

THE TOWER FROM THE SANDS 1894 34802

The Tower just prior to its opening. The owners planned to build a sister tower at Wembley Park, where Wembley Stadium now stands. The Blackpool Tower stress-diagrams were used as the basis for the new structure. Construction went ahead, but work had to be abandoned when the tower had reached 200ft, as one of the foundations had begun to sink.

FROM CENTRAL PIER 1896 38844

The reflections of the Tower and the sailing boats kiss the sea on a brilliantly sunny, flat-calm day. The picture was taken from the Central Pier, and contrasts wonderfully with the grey skies and high sea in the picture on page 33. Given their numbering in the archive, it is possible that these pictures were taken within hours of one another.

CENTRAL PROMENADE C1955 B116017

The most visitors to arrive on one day by train occurred in July 1945. With travel restrictions lifted, no less than 102,889 trippers passed through the town's three railway stations. No one knows how many others came by car, bus or motorcycle.

FROM CENTRAL PIER 1899 43333
This 518ft replica of the Eiffel Tower opened at Whitsuntide in 1894, having cost £250,000 to build. Several other resorts planned similar structures, but only New Brighton and Morecambe built anything.

THE TOWER AND CENTRAL PROMENADE c1955 B116021

Two of the 1930s-built Balloon double-decker trams near the Tower. In all, twenty-seven of these cars were built between 1934 and 1935. The first batch were known as 'Luxury Dreadnoughts', as they replaced the old Dreadnought trams that had been the mainstay of the summer traffic for thirty years.

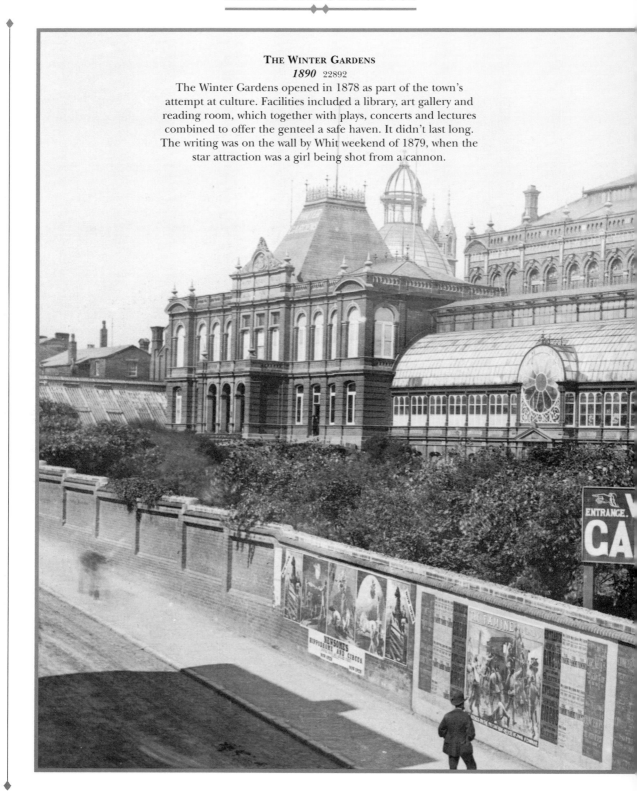

THE WINTER GARDENS
1890 22892

The Winter Gardens opened in 1878 as part of the town's
attempt at culture. Facilities included a library, art gallery and
reading room, which together with plays, concerts and lectures
combined to offer the genteel a safe haven. It didn't last long.
The writing was on the wall by Whit weekend of 1879, when the
star attraction was a girl being shot from a cannon.

THE WINTER GARDENS 1894 33954

Despite the grand appearance of the building, the acoustics in the Winter Gardens pavilion were suspect. When Sarah Bernhardt was engaged to play the female lead in 'The Lady of the Camellias', she had so much difficulty in making herself heard that she walked out at the end of the first act and never went back.

THE PALATINE HOTEL 1890 22891

The Palatine Hotel was one of the largest in the resort with 120 beds, though the Metropole and the hydropathic establishments were bigger. The County, Clifton, and Palatine were in a similar price range, and in 1906 their daily pension rate (room, meals and all services) was 8s 6d a day.

THE BIG WHEEL 1896 38865
Built next to the Winter Gardens in 1896 in an attempt to compete with the Tower, the 220ft Gigantic Wheel was a financial disaster. The ride cost 6d and lasted for one complete revolution of the wheel. However, every time one of the cars reached the bottom the wheel was stopped while it was unloaded and reloaded.

THE BIG WHEEL 1896 38867

THE BIG WHEEL 1896
Fancy a thing like this at the bottom of the garden? Each of the thirty cars held thirty passengers, and the ride lasted for about fifteen minutes. Losses were so great that as early as 1901 the Gardens seriously considered dismantling the brute, and were only stopped from doing so because the costs would prove prohibitive.

◆

ABINGDON STREET 1890
This photograph includes the Winter Gardens in the background. In 1887, William Holland was appointed manager. Holland had worked in the rough and tumble of the London music hall business, and his philosophy was simple: to give holiday makers the sort of entertainments they wanted, no matter how crass.

ABINGDON STREET 1890 22894

CHURCH STREET 1901 47039

James Duckworth Ltd, the grocery and provision chain, had a branch in this street, and others in Waterloo Road and Whitegate Drive. It was possible to place a grocery order at your local Duckworth branch, who would then arrange for one of the Blackpool shops to deliver it to your holiday accommodation in time for your arrival.

DEAN STREET 1901 47040

Most of the Wakes Week holiday-makers provided their own food, which was then cooked for them by the landlady; each room would have its own food locker in the dining room. There were plenty of inexpensive boarding houses charging only a shilling or two per night.

THE NURSES' HOME 1899 43480

This is the nurses' home at the local hospital. Nurses were unmarried and there were strict regulations governing their behaviour, both on and off duty. Gentlemen callers were not allowed beyond the foyer, under any circumstances whatsoever. Some nurses' homes even had resort to wrapping barbed wire around drainpipes.

CHRIST CHURCH 1890 22899

This church is noteable for its typically Victorian decorative brickwork.

CENTRAL PIER 1906 53855

The new pavilion on the Central Pier. It is hard to believe that when this pier was built, it was so far away from the town centre that the revenue it generated fell far short of what had been anticipated. To boost business, the pier operated excursions by steamer to Southport.

FROM SOUTH JETTY 1890 22868

As with many seaside resorts, one of the popular attractions was a trip in a boat. At Blackpool, sailing boats were often loaded and unloaded by means of portable gangways, one of which is in the picture. In the background is the North Pier, with an excursion steamer alongside its landing stage. This picture was taken from the South Jetty.

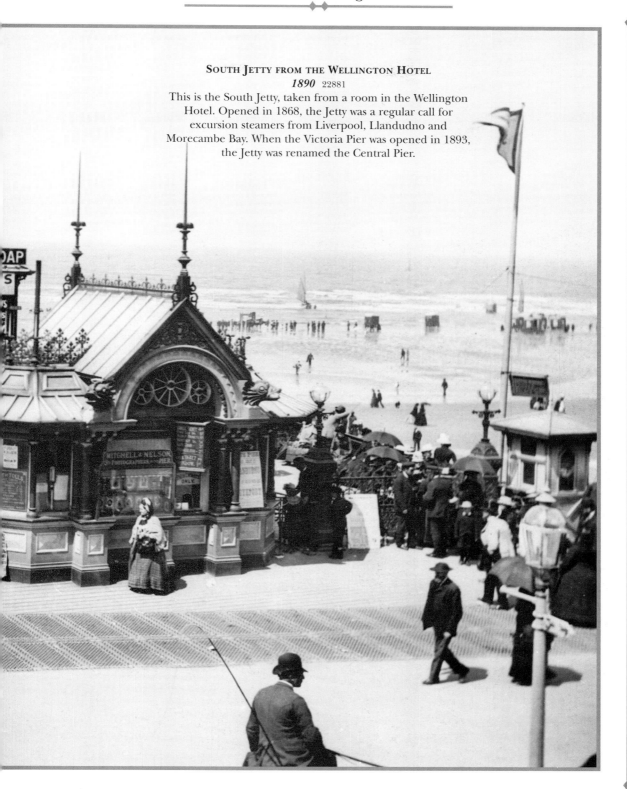

SOUTH JETTY FROM THE WELLINGTON HOTEL
1890 22881
This is the South Jetty, taken from a room in the Wellington Hotel. Opened in 1868, the Jetty was a regular call for excursion steamers from Liverpool, Llandudno and Morecambe Bay. When the Victoria Pier was opened in 1893, the Jetty was renamed the Central Pier.

CENTRAL BEACH 1890 22870
As well as portable gangways, boat carts were also used to get trippers to and from the sailing boats. In this picture, a boat-cart awaits the call to action, while the bathing machine concession has at least one paying customer in the water.

CENTRAL PIER 1896 38852

The tide is in, the sea is calm and the bathing machines have nowhere to go except on the Promenade. This picture was taken from the Central Pier and gives us an idea of what the town's sea defences looked like prior to the widening of the Promenade and the construction of the sea wall we all know and love today.

THE PROMENADE 1906 53869

A Dreadnought supertram rattles along the Promenade. These trams were capable of carrying 100 passengers; their unique design, with staircases either side of the driving positions, meant they could load and unload very quickly. During the season these trams operated with a crew of three: a driver and two conductors.

THE PROMENADE
1890 22875
Between the tramway tracks can be seen what appears to be
a third rail. This is the groove of the conduit system
through which the trams picked up current. Each tram was
fitted with a shoe that slotted into the groove and
connected with a live rail. The system was fraught with
difficulties owing to the conduit filling with drifting sand or
being flooded with sea water.

VIEW FROM THE PALATINE HOTEL 1890 22874
By the mid-1890s, most Lancashire cotton towns enjoyed a full Wakes Week. Places such as Blackburn and Burnley were all but empty as millworkers and their families escaped en masse to Blackpool, Southport, Morecambe, Scarborough and North Wales.

VIEW FROM THE PALATINE HOTEL 1906 53849
The most striking difference between this and the previous picture is the widening of the Promenade. The basic idea was to build a new sea wall, and then to pack the gap between it and the old defences with sand; the surface was then paved over.

THE ELECTRIC RAILCAR 1890 22873

The early tramway system suffered from heavy voltage loss due to inadequate insulation. This restricted the number of trams able to operate at any given time, and one of the measures taken to prevent the system from overloading was the introduction of a flat rate fare of 2d. This effectively put the trams beyond the pocket of many visitors.

FROM SOUTH PIER 1890 22872

A wagonette loaded with holiday-makers stands near Isaac Wilde's photography studio. Also in this block was Holden's dining rooms, Wolstenholmes (photographer to the Lord Mayor of London), Horace Fowler, who sold only non-alcoholic beer and soft drinks, and a place where you could hire tricycles.

THE SANDS 1896 38858
The tide is well and truly out. In those days, the beach area would often be a hive of activity, including donkey rides, ice cream and sweet stalls, shell fish and oyster sellers.

THE ESPLANADE 1890 22871
By the 1870s, many Lancashire cotton workers received three day's unpaid holiday a year, which was tacked onto a weekend to give a five-day break. Cheap rail fares and discounts at digs for block bookings boosted the holiday trade at both Blackpool and Southport.

CENTRAL PIER 1899 43331
Something is going on in the foreground. It might be a concert party - Pierrot troupes often put out chairs for small children - but it could just as easily be a beach mission or Sunday school outing.

THE SEA FRONT 1901 47034

THE SEA FRONT 1901

Wilfred Pickles used to tell a story about a mother and her son at a guest house. He had a broad accent, which embarrassed his mum. The little lad opened his mouth, but his mother guessed what he wanted and whispered 'Go upstairs, love. You know where it is'. A few seconds later there was a loud 'Mum!' from upstairs. 'I can see t'Tower while I'm on t'closet!'

THE SOUTH SHORE 1901

Blackpool's first tramway along the sea front was single track for the most part; there were passing loops every three hundred yards. Here we can see where the conduit ran between the lines. By this date it had been filled in, and the system converted to overhead supply.

THE SOUTH SHORE 1901 47036

THE SEA FRONT 1901 47037

At the time when this picture was taken, a holiday in Blackpool represented a considerable outlay for the average factory or mill worker. There was no such thing as holiday pay, and wouldn't be until the 1930s. One way of saving was by making weekly payments into a holiday club.

THE FLYING MACHINE
1906 53857
The Pleasure Beach actually started as a fairground on the South Shore. One of the early rides was the Sir Hiram Maxim Flying Machine. The ride was built in 1904, and hurtled round at an exhilarating 40mph.

THE PARADE 1896 38859

THE PARADE 1896
The tide is on its way out and people are beginning to wander onto the beach. We have no record of what the tents were being used for; the nearest appears to have a signboard outside it, while the farthest one could be selling tea or coffee.

THE VICTORIA PIER 1894
The Victoria Pier about a year after it had opened. A large pavilion was later built near the entrance to provide additional facilities, and the name was changed to the South Pier.

THE VICTORIA PIER 1894 33951

CORPORATION PARK 1899 43483

Another park, Raikes Hall, was established in 1871 and included formal gardens, an aquarium, concert hall and refreshment rooms. In 1874, after a liquor licence was granted for the whole park, any pretence at the place being for the genteel set was lost. From then onwards, the park changed and flower beds were replaced with fairground rides.

FLEETWOOD, GENERAL VIEW 1898 41015

Construction of the American-influenced Blackpool & Fleetwood Tramroad (B&FT) began in July 1897, and by September 1898 the line was fully opened. From Ash Street to the Blackpool terminus at Gynn, the tramroad ran on a reserved track segregated from other road traffic; it was only at the northern end that it actually ran through the streets of Fleetwood.

FLEETWOOD, EAST STREET 1898 47074
Pictured here is one of ten American-style, 48-seat enclosed cars supplied by Milnes & Co, which were fitted with controllers and motors supplied by General Electric of the USA.

FLEETWOOD, RAILWAY STATION AND LIGHTHOUSE 1898 47079
Over on the left is the Lancashire & Yorkshire and London & North Western joint railway station, which was conveniently built next to the steamer berths. On the right is one of the town's landmarks, the Pharos Lighthouse.

FLEETWOOD, THE MOUNT HOTEL 1901 47072
Fleetwood's other principal hotel was the Mount. The hotel was built with its front on the promenade, offering guests excellent views of the bay.

FLEETWOOD, THE PIER 1918 68413
The pier was considerably shorter in length than those at Blackpool, but somewhat similar in design to the one at Aberystwyth.

FLEETWOOD
The Lower Promenade 1898
The lower promenade, with the North Euston Hotel, owned by the London & North Western Railway, in the background. Also featured is the landing-stage for the ferry to Knott End-on-Sea.

FLEETWOOD
The Ferry 1901
Visit any resort where there are fishing vessels and you will be sure to find plenty of onlookers. In the distance is the landing stage at Knott End-on-Sea. For years, the service was worked by two boats, the 'Progress' and the 'Wyresdale'.

FLEETWOOD, THE LOWER PROMENADE 1898 41009

FLEETWOOD, THE FERRY 1901 47069

FLEETWOOD, THE BEACH 1902 49051
Holiday-makers gather round one of the seaside entertainments. Unfortunately, we have no idea what they were watching, as the Frith cameraman didn't bother to record the details. It could be a Pierrot troupe, or even a minstrel show; both of these were popular acts at the time.

FLEETWOOD
The 'Viking' 1908 59939
The turbine steamer 'Viking', departing for
Douglas. When this picture was taken the turbine
steamers were usually assigned to the
Liverpool-Douglas and Heysham-Douglas
services. It was also possible to sail to Douglas
from Barrow, Silloth, Whitehaven and Glasgow.

FLEETWOOD, 'MONA'S QUEEN' 1904 52171
The 'Mona's Queen', which belonged to the Isle of Man Steam Packet Co, eases out of Fleetwood for a summer sailing. The crossing to the Isle of Man took about three hours; the daily sailing was scheduled to leave after the arrival of the 2.15pm train. There was also a twice-weekly sailing to Ramsey via Douglas.

FLEETWOOD, THE BARROW BOAT 1908 59940
The Furness Railway paddle-steamer 'Philomel' entering Fleetwood. Built in 1899 for the General Steam Navigation Co, the paddler was purchased by the Furness Railway in 1907. It entered service on the Barrow-Fleetwood run in April 1908.

FLEETWOOD, THE HARBOUR 1894 33968

It was here in 1847 that Queen Victoria first set foot in Lancashire, when she arrived at the harbour having travelled from Scotland by sea. The remainder of her journey was by train. Prince Albert had travelled by train in 1839, but it was not until 1842 that Victoria could be persuaded to take the train from Windsor to London.

CLEVELEYS, THE ARENA AND PROMENADE c1955 C440009

Cleveleys is the most northerly, from Blackpool, of the small resorts leading up to Fleetwood. Though the resort was away from the railway, holiday-makers could easily reach it by tram, either from Fleetwood or from North Station. One of the earliest Corporation bus services was the Cleveleys to Thornton route, which began operating in July 1921.

LYTHAM
Minstrel Show 1914 67479
Modern minstrel shows originated in the USA
during the early 19th century, possibly the 1840s,
with a troupe called the Christie Minstrels. The
entertainers usually, but not necessarily, wore
blackface makeup, sang songs and told jokes.

LYTHAM, DONKEY RIDES 1914 67480
Time for a donkey ride, sweets and ice cream. The summer of 1914 was long and hot; the hottest day of the year in Lancashire was 28 June.

LYTHAM, THE PIER 1913 66439

At this time the resident population was around 9,000, compared to 58,000 for Blackpool. Even after amalgamating with St Anne's, the town continued to maintain its status as a quiet residential resort.

LYTHAM, FROM THE PIER 1907 59120

The town was well laid-out, and there were plenty of opulent villas available for those merchants and industrialists who preferred to live by the sea and commute.

LYTHAM, THE PIER 1921 70740
Though well-maintained and kept in top-flight condition, Lytham Pier was of a somewhat functional design when compared to the one at St Anne's, or to the South Pier at Blackpool.

LYTHAM, THE BEACH FROM THE PIER 1901 47085

The children's amusements at Lytham consisted of a few swings, donkey rides and a couple of stalls. There is quite a large crowd gathered down toward the old windmill. Unfortunately, we have no idea what is going on, but it is reasonable to assume that it is a concert.

LYTHAM, FROM THE PIER 1894 33958

The same view as the previous picture. These two pictures give us some idea of the different philosophies behind the development of the Fylde resorts.

LYTHAM, MARKET SQUARE 1907 59131

LYTHAM
Market Square 1907
A Blackpool-bound tram pulls into the Market Square. Through-services to Blackpool began in 1897, and the route was via St Anne's, then along through the sand dunes of Clifton Drive, then to Squires Gate, and on to Station Road.

◆

LYTHAM
The Town Hall and Fountain 1890
This classical-style brick building, with its heavy rustication, manages to look light-hearted, thanks to its cupola. It is a hot, sunny day and one of the tourists is putting up her parasol.

LYTHAM, THE TOWN HALL AND FOUNTAIN 1890 22905

LYTHAM, CLIFTON STREET 1901 47082
At this time the 20-bed Ship & Royal Hotel on Clifton Street (the telephone number was 186) was one of two Lytham hotels recommended by the AA. The other one was the Clifton Arms.

LYTHAM, CLIFTON STREET 1907 59132
The tramway was only electrified in 1903. Until then it had operated using gas-propelled trams. The gas was stored in reservoirs which gave sufficient fuel for sixteen miles. The gas trams were far from satisfactory, with the result that in 1900 twenty horse-trams were also acquired.

LYTHAM
Clifton Street 1923 74193
On the right, Parkinsons shop is a typical grocer's
shop in the old style, selling everything from tea
to motor tours. Its frontage is smothered with
famous old trade names including Cadburys,
Lyons, St Bruno and St Julien.

LYTHAM, CLIFTON STREET 1907 59133
There was a scheme to extend the tramway all the way to Preston via Freckleton. The only section to be built was a 1,100-yard single line from the terminus at Lytham to East Beach.

ST ANNE'S, ST ANNE'S ROAD 1913 66474
This photograph looks towards the seafront and the pier. Though there are one or two motorcars around, the scene is relatively traffic free; people appear to be quite at ease either walking or standing in the middle of the road.

ST ANNE'S, ORCHARD ROAD 1901 47091
The other side of the street. The hardware store has had a pre-season facelift: a new awning, a coat of paint, and the relocation of the shop-sign from the ground to the second floor.

St Anne's
The Boat Trips 1914 67490
Against a backdrop provided by the pier pavilion and
landing stage, St Anne's boatmen are doing a brisk
trade taking holiday-makers out for a trip around the
bay. It is the long, hot summer of 1914 and, for
young gentlemen, sailor's suits complete with silks
and lanyards are the order of the day.

ST ANNE'S, SOUTH DRIVE 1914 67487
Tramcar No. 23 trundles along South Drive on its way to Lytham. The paving blocks between the tracks were made from white wood, balastic lava or jarrah. The running of connecting trams between Lytham and Blackpool began in 1905.

ST ANNE'S, THE SQUARE 1921 70745
The Square has a French-sounding hairdresser's salon, a quality grocery store, and superbly-kept flower beds. The huge advertising signs above the grocer's and shoe shop would not be allowed today.

ST ANNE'S, THE BOATING POOL 1918 68340
The 1921 edition of the Dunlop book recommended three St Anne's hotels as being suitable for those on motoring holidays. There was the 260-bed Imperial Hydro (telephone, 258) with garage space for fifty automobiles, the Grand (telephone, 55) and the Station.

ST ANNE'S, THE PIER 1906 53887
The design reflects a number of different styles: a mock-Tudor entrance, Chinese pavilions and an Indian-influenced palace. It must have looked superb when first opened.

ST ANNE'S, ON THE PIER 1906 53888
Out for a stroll on a sunny summer afternoon. The pier is in immaculate condition, but then this is before the days of discarded ice cream wrappers, coke and beer cans, and anything else you care to think of.

ST ANNE'S, THE PIER PAVILION 1906 53890
This exotic architectural confection reminds us of the Pavilion at Brighton, with its oriental domes and minarets. It must have seemed like something out of 'The Arabian Nights' to the average Victorian holidaymaker.

ST ANNE'S, THE ROYAL LYTHAM GOLF CLUB HOUSE 1901 47106
By 1921 the green fees at the Old Links, St Anne's were 2s 6d on weekdays and higher at weekends, whilst the Lytham & St Anne's club charged a fee of 5s for play on any day of the week.

FAIRHAVEN, THE LAKE 1923 74203
At Fairhaven, visitors could take their exercise pulling on the oars of a rowing boat or playing 18 holes on the local golf course. Along with the Old Links and the Lytham & St Anne's, the Fairhaven was open to members of the Ladies' Golf Union. The Fairhaven was the only club on the Fylde coast that closed on Sundays.

Index

Frith Book Co Titles

www.francisfrith.co.uk

The Frith Book Company publishes over 100 new titles each year. A selection of those currently available are listed below. For latest catalogue please contact Frith Book Co.

Town Books 96pages, approx 100 photos. County and Themed Books 128 pages, approx 150 photos (unless specified). All titles hardback laminated case and jacket except those indicated pb (paperback)

Amersham, Chesham & Rickmansworth (pb)			Derby (pb)	1-85937-367-4	£9.99
	1-85937-340-2	£9.99	Derbyshire (pb)	1-85937-196-5	£9.99
Ancient Monuments & Stone Circles	1-85937-143-4	£17.99	Devon (pb)	1-85937-297-x	£9.99
Aylesbury (pb)	1-85937-227-9	£9.99	Dorset (pb)	1-85937-269-4	£9.99
Bakewell	1-85937-113-2	£12.99	Dorset Churches	1-85937-172-8	£17.99
Barnstaple (pb)	1-85937-300-3	£9.99	Dorset Coast (pb)	1-85937-299-6	£9.99
Bath (pb)	1-85937419-0	£9.99	Dorset Living Memories	1-85937-210-4	£14.99
Bedford (pb)	1-85937-205-8	£9.99	Down the Severn	1-85937-118-3	£14.99
Berkshire (pb)	1-85937-191-4	£9.99	Down the Thames (pb)	1-85937-278-3	£9.99
Berkshire Churches	1-85937-170-1	£17.99	Down the Trent	1-85937-311-9	£14.99
Blackpool (pb)	1-85937-382-8	£9.99	Dublin (pb)	1-85937-231-7	£9.99
Bognor Regis (pb)	1-85937-431-x	£9.99	East Anglia (pb)	1-85937-265-1	£9.99
Bournemouth	1-85937-067-5	£12.99	East London	1-85937-080-2	£14.99
Bradford (pb)	1-85937-204-x	£9.99	East Sussex	1-85937-130-2	£14.99
Brighton & Hove(pb)	1-85937-192-2	£8.99	Eastbourne	1-85937-061-6	£12.99
Bristol (pb)	1-85937-264-3	£9.99	Edinburgh (pb)	1-85937-193-0	£8.99
British Life A Century Ago (pb)	1-85937-213-9	£9.99	England in the 1880s	1-85937-331-3	£17.99
Buckinghamshire (pb)	1-85937-200-7	£9.99	English Castles (pb)	1-85937-434-4	£9.99
Camberley (pb)	1-85937-222-8	£9.99	English Country Houses	1-85937-161-2	£17.99
Cambridge (pb)	1-85937-422-0	£9.99	Essex (pb)	1-85937-270-8	£9.99
Cambridgeshire (pb)	1-85937-420-4	£9.99	Exeter	1-85937-126-4	£12.99
Canals & Waterways (pb)	1-85937-291-0	£9.99	Exmoor	1-85937-132-9	£14.99
Canterbury Cathedral (pb)	1-85937-179-5	£9.99	Falmouth	1-85937-066-7	£12.99
Cardiff (pb)	1-85937-093-4	£9.99	Folkestone (pb)	1-85937-124-8	£9.99
Carmarthenshire	1-85937-216-3	£14.99	Glasgow (pb)	1-85937-190-6	£9.99
Chelmsford (pb)	1-85937-310-0	£9.99	Gloucestershire	1-85937-102-7	£14.99
Cheltenham (pb)	1-85937-095-0	£9.99	Great Yarmouth (pb)	1-85937-426-3	£9.99
Cheshire (pb)	1-85937-271-6	£9.99	Greater Manchester (pb)	1-85937-266-x	£9.99
Chester	1-85937-090-x	£12.99	Guildford (pb)	1-85937-410-7	£9.99
Chesterfield	1-85937-378-x	£9.99	Hampshire (pb)	1-85937-279-1	£9.99
Chichester (pb)	1-85937-228-7	£9.99	Hampshire Churches (pb)	1-85937-207-4	£9.99
Colchester (pb)	1-85937-188-4	£8.99	Harrogate	1-85937-423-9	£9.99
Cornish Coast	1-85937-163-9	£14.99	Hastings & Bexhill (pb)	1-85937-131-0	£9.99
Cornwall (pb)	1-85937-229-5	£9.99	Heart of Lancashire (pb)	1-85937-197-3	£9.99
Cornwall Living Memories	1-85937-248-1	£14.99	Helston (pb)	1-85937-214-7	£9.99
Cotswolds (pb)	1-85937-230-9	£9.99	Hereford (pb)	1-85937-175-2	£9.99
Cotswolds Living Memories	1-85937-255-4	£14.99	Herefordshire	1-85937-174-4	£14.99
County Durham	1-85937-123-x	£14.99	Hertfordshire (pb)	1-85937-247-3	£9.99
Croydon Living Memories	1-85937-162-0	£9.99	Horsham (pb)	1-85937-432-8	£9.99
Cumbria	1-85937-101-9	£14.99	Humberside	1-85937-215-5	£14.99
Dartmoor	1-85937-145-0	£14.99	Hythe, Romney Marsh & Ashford	1-85937-256-2	£9.99

Available from your local bookshop or from the publisher

Frith Book Co Titles (continued)

Title	ISBN	Price	Title	ISBN	Price
Ipswich (pb)	1-85937-424-7	£9.99	St Ives (pb)	1-85937415-8	£9.99
Ireland (pb)	1-85937-181-7	£9.99	Scotland (pb)	1-85937-182-5	£9.99
Isle of Man (pb)	1-85937-268-6	£9.99	Scottish Castles (pb)	1-85937-323-2	£9.99
Isles of Scilly	1-85937-136-1	£14.99	Sevenoaks & Tunbridge	1-85937-057-8	£12.99
Isle of Wight (pb)	1-85937-429-8	£9.99	Sheffield, South Yorks (pb)	1-85937-267-8	£9.99
Isle of Wight Living Memories	1-85937-304-6	£14.99	Shrewsbury (pb)	1-85937-325-9	£9.99
Kent (pb)	1-85937-189-2	£9.99	Shropshire (pb)	1-85937-326-7	£9.99
Kent Living Memories	1-85937-125-6	£14.99	Somerset	1-85937-153-1	£14.99
Lake District (pb)	1-85937-275-9	£9.99	South Devon Coast	1-85937-107-8	£14.99
Lancaster, Morecambe & Heysham (pb)	1-85937-233-3	£9.99	South Devon Living Memories	1-85937-168-x	£14.99
Leeds (pb)	1-85937-202-3	£9.99	South Hams	1-85937-220-1	£14.99
Leicester	1-85937-073-x	£12.99	Southampton (pb)	1-85937-427-1	£9.99
Leicestershire (pb)	1-85937-185-x	£9.99	Southport (pb)	1-85937-425-5	£9.99
Lincolnshire (pb)	1-85937-433-6	£9.99	Staffordshire	1-85937-047-0	£12.99
Liverpool & Merseyside (pb)	1-85937-234-1	£9.99	Stratford upon Avon	1-85937-098-5	£12.99
London (pb)	1-85937-183-3	£9.99	Suffolk (pb)	1-85937-221-x	£9.99
Ludlow (pb)	1-85937-176-0	£9.99	Suffolk Coast	1-85937-259-7	£14.99
Luton (pb)	1-85937-235-x	£9.99	Surrey (pb)	1-85937-240-6	£9.99
Maidstone	1-85937-056-x	£14.99	Sussex (pb)	1-85937-184-1	£9.99
Manchester (pb)	1-85937-198-1	£9.99	Swansea (pb)	1-85937-167-1	£9.99
Middlesex	1-85937-158-2	£14.99	Tees Valley & Cleveland	1-85937-211-2	£14.99
New Forest	1-85937-128-0	£14.99	Thanet (pb)	1-85937-116-7	£9.99
Newark (pb)	1-85937-366-6	£9.99	Tiverton (pb)	1-85937-178-7	£9.99
Newport, Wales (pb)	1-85937-258-9	£9.99	Torbay	1-85937-063-2	£12.99
Newquay (pb)	1-85937-421-2	£9.99	Truro	1-85937-147-7	£12.99
Norfolk (pb)	1-85937-195-7	£9.99	Victorian and Edwardian Cornwall	1-85937-252-x	£14.99
Norfolk Living Memories	1-85937-217-1	£14.99	Victorian & Edwardian Devon	1-85937-253-8	£14.99
Northamptonshire	1-85937-150-7	£14.99	Victorian & Edwardian Kent	1-85937-149-3	£14.99
Northumberland Tyne & Wear (pb)	1-85937-281-3	£9.99	Vic & Ed Maritime Album	1-85937-144-2	£17.99
North Devon Coast	1-85937-146-9	£14.99	Victorian and Edwardian Sussex	1-85937-157-4	£14.99
North Devon Living Memories	1-85937-261-9	£14.99	Victorian & Edwardian Yorkshire	1-85937-154-x	£14.99
North London	1-85937-206-6	£14.99	Victorian Seaside	1-85937-159-0	£17.99
North Wales (pb)	1-85937-298-8	£9.99	Villages of Devon (pb)	1-85937-293-7	£9.99
North Yorkshire (pb)	1-85937-236-8	£9.99	Villages of Kent (pb)	1-85937-294-5	£9.99
Norwich (pb)	1-85937-194-9	£8.99	Villages of Sussex (pb)	1-85937-295-3	£9.99
Nottingham (pb)	1-85937-324-0	£9.99	Warwickshire (pb)	1-85937-203-1	£9.99
Nottinghamshire (pb)	1-85937-187-6	£9.99	Welsh Castles (pb)	1-85937-322-4	£9.99
Oxford (pb)	1-85937-411-5	£9.99	West Midlands (pb)	1-85937-289-9	£9.99
Oxfordshire (pb)	1-85937-430-1	£9.99	West Sussex	1-85937-148-5	£14.99
Peak District (pb)	1-85937-280-5	£9.99	West Yorkshire (pb)	1-85937-201-5	£9.99
Penzance	1-85937-069-1	£12.99	Weymouth (pb)	1-85937-209-0	£9.99
Peterborough (pb)	1-85937-219-8	£9.99	Wiltshire (pb)	1-85937-277-5	£9.99
Piers	1-85937-237-6	£17.99	Wiltshire Churches (pb)	1-85937-171-x	£9.99
Plymouth	1-85937-119-1	£12.99	Wiltshire Living Memories	1-85937-245-7	£14.99
Poole & Sandbanks (pb)	1-85937-251-1	£9.99	Winchester (pb)	1-85937-428-x	£9.99
Preston (pb)	1-85937-212-0	£9.99	Windmills & Watermills	1-85937-242-2	£17.99
Reading (pb)	1-85937-238-4	£9.99	Worcester (pb)	1-85937-165-5	£9.99
Romford (pb)	1-85937-319-4	£9.99	Worcestershire	1-85937-152-3	£14.99
Salisbury (pb)	1-85937-239-2	£9.99	York (pb)	1-85937-199-x	£9.99
Scarborough (pb)	1-85937-379-8	£9.99	Yorkshire (pb)	1-85937-186-8	£9.99
St Albans (pb)	1-85937-341-0	£9.99	Yorkshire Living Memories	1-85937-166-3	£14.99

See Frith books on the internet www.francisfrith.co.uk

FRITH PRODUCTS & SERVICES

Francis Frith would doubtless be pleased to know that the pioneering publishing venture he started in 1860 still continues today. A hundred and forty years later, The Francis Frith Collection continues in the same innovative tradition and is now one of the foremost publishers of vintage photographs in the world. Some of the current activities include:

Interior Decoration

Today Frith's photographs can be seen framed and as giant wall murals in thousands of pubs, restaurants, hotels, banks, retail stores and other public buildings throughout the country. In every case they enhance the unique local atmosphere of the places they depict and provide reminders of gentler days in an increasingly busy and frenetic world.

Product Promotions

Frith products are used by many major companies to promote the sales of their own products or to reinforce their own history and heritage. Frith promotions have been used by Hovis bread, Courage beers, Scots Porage Oats, Colman's mustard, Cadbury's foods, Mellow Birds coffee, Dunhill pipe tobacco, Guinness, and Bulmer's Cider.

Genealogy and Family History

As the interest in family history and roots grows world-wide, more and more people are turning to Frith's photographs of Great Britain for images of the towns, villages and streets where their ancestors lived; and, of course, photographs of the churches and chapels where their ancestors were christened, married and buried are an essential part of every genealogy tree and family album.

Frith Products

All Frith photographs are available Framed or just as Mounted Prints and Posters (size 23 x 16 inches). These may be ordered from the address below. From time to time other products - Address Books, Calendars, Table Mats, etc - are available.

The Internet

Already twenty thousand Frith photographs can be viewed and purchased on the internet through the Frith websites and a myriad of partner sites.

For more detailed information on Frith companies and products, look at these sites:

www.francisfrith.co.uk
www.francisfrith.com
(for North American visitors)

See the complete list of Frith Books at:

www.francisfrith.co.uk

This web site is regularly updated with the latest list of publications from the Frith Book Company. If you wish to buy books relating to another part of the country that your local bookshop does not stock, you may purchase on-line.

For further information, trade, or author enquiries please contact us at the address below:
The Francis Frith Collection, Frith's Barn, Teffont, Salisbury, Wiltshire, England SP3 5QP.
Tel: +44 (0)1722 716 376 Fax: +44 (0)1722 716 881 Email: sales@francisfrith.co.uk

See Frith books on the internet www.francisfrith.co.uk

TO RECEIVE YOUR FREE MOUNTED PRINT

Mounted Print
Overall size 14 x 11 inches

Cut out this Voucher and return it with your remittance for £1.95 to cover postage and handling, to UK addresses. For overseas addresses please include £4.00 post and handling. Choose any photograph included in this book. Your SEPIA print will be A4 in size, and mounted in a cream mount with burgundy rule line, overall size 14 x 11 inches.

Order additional Mounted Prints at HALF PRICE (only £7.49 each*)

If there are further pictures you would like to order, possibly as gifts for friends and family, purchase them at half price (no additional postage and handling required).

Have your Mounted Prints framed*

For an additional £14.95 per print you can have your chosen Mounted Print framed in an elegant polished wood and gilt moulding, overall size 16 x 13 inches (no additional postage and handling required).

> *** IMPORTANT!**
> These special prices are only available if ordered using the original voucher on this page (no copies permitted) and at the same time as your free Mounted Print, for delivery to the same address

Frith Collectors' Guild

From time to time we publish a magazine of news and stories about Frith photographs and further special offers of Frith products. If you would like 12 months FREE membership, please return this form.

Send completed forms to:
The Francis Frith Collection, Frith's Barn, Teffont, Salisbury, Wiltshire SP3 5QP

Voucher for FREE and Reduced Price Frith Prints

Picture no.	Page number	Qty	Mounted @ £7.49	Framed + £14.95	Total Cost
		1	**Free of charge***	£	£
			£7.49	£	£
			£7.49	£	£
			£7.49	£	£
			£7.49	£	£
			£7.49	£	£

Please allow 28 days for delivery	*** Post & handling**	**£1.95**
Book Title	**Total Order Cost**	**£**

Please do not photocopy this voucher. Only the original is valid, so please cut it out and return it to us.

I enclose a cheque / postal order for £ . . . . made payable to 'The Francis Frith Collection'
OR please debit my Mastercard / Visa / Switch / Amex card *(credit cards please on all overseas orders)*

Number . . . .

Issue No(Switch only) . . . . .Valid from (Amex/Switch) . . . .

Expires . . . . Signature . . . .

Name Mr/Mrs/Ms . . . .

Address . . . .

. . . .

. . . . Postcode . . . .

Daytime Tel No . . . .   Valid to 31/12/02

The Francis Frith Collectors' Guild

Please enrol me as a member for 12 months free of charge.

Name Mr/Mrs/Ms . . . .

Address . . . .

. . . .

. . . . Postcode . . . .

Would you like to find out more about Francis Frith?

We have recently recruited some entertaining speakers who are happy to visit local groups, clubs and societies to give an illustrated talk documenting Frith's travels and photographs. If you are a member of such a group and are interested in hosting a presentation, we would love to hear from you.

Our speakers bring with them a small selection of our local town and county books, together with sample prints. They are happy to take orders. A small proportion of the order value is donated to the group who have hosted the presentation. The talks are therefore an excellent way of fundraising for small groups and societies.

Can you help us with information about any of the Frith photographs in this book?

We are gradually compiling an historical record for each of the photographs in the Frith archive. It is always fascinating to find out the names of the people shown in the pictures, as well as insights into the shops, buildings and other features depicted.

If you recognize anyone in the photographs in this book, or if you have information not already included in the author's caption, do let us know. We would love to hear from you, and will try to publish it in future books or articles.

Our production team

Frith books are produced by a small dedicated team at offices in the converted Grade II listed 18th-century barn at Teffont near Salisbury, illustrated above. Most have worked with the Frith Collection for many years. All have in common one quality: they have a passion for the Frith Collection. The team is constantly expanding, but currently includes:

Jason Buck, John Buck, Douglas Burns, Heather Crisp, Isobel Hall, Rob Hames, Hazel Heaton, Peter Horne, James Kinnear, Tina Leary, Hannah Marsh, Eliza Sackett, Terence Sackett, Sandra Sanger, Shelley Tolcher, Susanna Walker, Clive Wathen and Jenny Wathen.